CARMEN SÆCULARE

A JUBILEE ODE

BY

ALFRED TENNYSON, D.C.L.

Poet Laureate

188-

TENNYSON

Published April 15th 8? by Macmillan & Co 35 New Bond St

CARMEN SÆCULARE

CARMEN SÆCULARE

AN ODE

BY

ALFRED TENNYSON, D.C.L.

Poet Laureate

LONDON

PRINTED FOR PRIVATE DISTRIBUTION

1887

CARMEN SÆCULARE

A JUBILEE ODE

I

FIFTY times the rose has flower'd and
    faded,
Fifty times the golden harvest fallen,
Since our Queen assumed the globe, the
    sceptre.

II

She beloved for a kindliness
Rare in Fable or History,
Queen, and Empress of India,
Crown'd so long with a diadem
Never worn by a worthier,
Now with prosperous auguries
Comes at last to the bounteous
Crowning year of her Jubilee.

III

Nothing of the lawless, of the Despot,
Nothing of the vulgar, or vainglorious,
All is gracious, gentle, great and Queenly.

IV

You then joyfully, all of you,
Set the mountain aflame to-night,
Shoot your stars to the firmament,
Deck your houses, illuminate
All your towns for a festival,
And in each let a multitude
Loyal, each, to the heart of it,
One full voice of allegiance,
Hail the fair Ceremonial
Of this year of her Jubilee.

V

Queen, as true to womanhood as Queen-
    hood,
Glorying in the glories of her people,
Sorrowing with the sorrows of the lowest!

VI

You, that wanton in affluence,
Spare not now to be bountiful,
Call your poor to regale with you,
All the lowly, the destitute,
Make their neighbourhood healthfuller,
Give your gold to the Hospital,
Let the weary be comforted,
Let the needy be banqueted,
Let the maim'd in his heart rejoice
At this glad Ceremonial,
And this year of her Jubilee.

VII

Henry's fifty years are all in shadow,
Gray with distance Edward's fifty sum-
    mers,
Ev'n her Grandsire's fifty half forgotten.

VIII

You, the Patriot Architect,
You that shape for Eternity,
Raise a stately memorial,
Make it really gorgeous,
Some Imperial Institute,
Rich in symbol, in ornament,
Which may speak to the centuries,
All the centuries after us,
Of this great Ceremonial,
And this year of her Jubilee.

IX

Fifty years of ever-broadening Com-
    merce !
Fifty years of ever-brightening Science !
Fifty years of ever-widening Empire !

X

You, the Mighty, the Fortunate,
You, the Lord-territorial,
You, the Lord-manufacturer,
You, the hardy, laborious,
Patient children of Albion,
You, Canadian, Indian,
Australasian, African,
All your hearts be in harmony,
All your voices in unison,
Singing " Hail to the glorious
Golden year of her Jubilee ! "

XI

Are there thunders moaning in the dis-
    tance ?
Are there spectres moving in the dark-
    ness ?
Trust the Hand of Light will lead her
    people,
Till the thunders pass, the spectres vanish,
And the Light is Victor, and the darkness
Dawns into the Jubilee of the Ages.